A Star in My Heart

A Mother's Love That Still Shines Bright After She's Gone

Michelle Huirama

To every brave child learning to live with a missing piece—

Your Mom's love didn't disappear.

il became a light inside you.

May you carry it proudly, gently, and always.

Book Cover by Tukotuku Publishing

Illustrations by Tukotuku Publishing

First edition 2025

Print ISBN: 978-1-991366-01-6

Ebook ISBN: 978-1-991366-02-3

TUKOTUKU PUBLISHING

Contents

Hello There

Hi,

If you're reading this, it might mean you've lost your Mom. And that's one of the hardest things a heart can go through.

This book was written just for you—to help you feel less alone, to remind you that it's okay to feel sad (or mad or confused), and to help you remember that your Mom's love didn't disappear.

It's still inside you. Always.

In these pages, you'll find stories, ideas, and gentle ways to remember her. You'll learn that grief is not about forgetting—it's about holding on to love in a new way.

Understanding Loss

Chapter 1- What Happened to Mom?

In this chapter, we will learn about what it means to lose someone we love, like Mom, and how to understand all the big feelings that come with it.

We'll talk about the questions you might have, the ways your heart might hurt, and why it's okay to feel sad or even angry. You'll also discover who you can talk to and how asking for help is a brave thing to do. Remember, even when it feels like everything has changed, Mom's love is still with you — always, right there in your heart.

When someone we love dies, like our Mom, it can feel like the world has changed forever. You might feel like there's a big empty space in your heart where her hugs used to be. That's okay. Missing her is part of loving her.

Sometimes, you might wonder: Where did she go? Why can't I see her anymore? These questions are normal. Grown-ups might say she went to heaven, became a star, or lives in your heart now. You can believe what feels right for you.

Even though Mom isn't here in the same way, her love is still with you. Every kind word she said, every bedtime story, every hug—those stay in your heart forever.

It's Okay to Feel Sad

You might feel like crying. Or you might not. You could feel mad, confused, quiet, or even laugh when you remember something funny. All of those feelings are normal.

Grief is like a rollercoaster with lots of ups and downs. Some days feel okay, others feel heavy. But just like the weather changes, your feelings will too. And that's completely normal.

Who Can Help Me?

You don't have to go through this alone. You can talk to someone you trust—like your dad, a caregiver,a grandparent, a teacher, or a school counselor.

You can also write down your thoughts or draw pictures when your feelings are too big to talk about.

Remember, asking for help is brave. There are people who care about you and want to listen.

Reflection 1

Understanding Loss

What are some things you remember most about your Mom?

1. **Draw a picture of something special you and Mom loved doing together.**
   Maybe it was baking, reading, or walking in the park — your drawing can help you remember those moments with a smile.

2. Write down your favorite thing about Mom.

Was it her laugh? The way she hugged you? Her kind words? Write one or more things that made her feel so special to you.

3. Think about a time Mom helped you feel brave or safe.

Can you tell or write that story? How did it make you feel?

4. List three things Mom taught you.

They could be simple — like how to tie your shoes — or big — like how to be kind.

1.

2.

3.

5. Describe a time when Mom made you laugh.

You can write about it, draw it, or even act it out with someone you trust.

Todays Date:

My Feelings Today

Circle how you're feeling right now (you can choose more than one):

Happy   Sad   Angry   Confused
Calm   Missing Mom   Loved

Then write or draw about your feelings below

Reflection 2

2. Sometimes, when you miss your mom, drawing can help you feel close to her again. Take out your favorite pencils or markers and think of a happy moment you shared. Maybe you baked cookies together, played in the garden, read a bedtime story, or went for a walk in the park. Picture her smile, her laugh, and how warm you felt being with her.

On your paper, draw the two of you doing that special thing. You can include lots of details—like the color of her shirt, the flowers you saw, the cookies you made, or the books you read. You could even draw speech bubbles with things you both might have said, like "I love you!" or "This is so fun!"

When you finish, look at your drawing and think about how it makes your heart feel. Maybe you feel warm and happy remembering, or maybe a little sad because you miss her. That's okay—both feelings can live together.

If you'd like, you can hang up your drawing somewhere special, like on your bedroom wall or in a memory box, so you can see it whenever you want to remember that happy time. Your drawing is a way of keeping that love close and reminding yourself that

Mom's love will always be part of you, no matter what.

MICHELLE HUIRAMA

Todays Date:

My Feelings Today

Circle how you're feeling right now (you can choose more than one):

Happy   Sad   Angry   Confused
Calm   Missing Mom   Loved

Then write or draw about your feelings below

Reflection 3

3. What does 'grief' mean to you? How does it feel in your body?

Grief is a word we use for the deep, big feelings we have when someone we love is gone. But what does grief feel like to you? Take a moment to think about it. Does it feel heavy, like carrying a big backpack? Or does it feel like a raincloud over your head? Maybe it feels like a knot in your tummy or like tears that come without warning.

Sometimes grief can even feel like missing hugs, or like your heart is a little empty where love used to live. Other times, it might feel quiet and far away, or confusing, with lots of different feelings at the same time.

You can write about how grief feels for you, using words like "sad," "angry," "lonely," "worried," or even "confused." Or, if you'd rather, you can draw a picture to show what grief feels like. Maybe you'll draw a stormy sky, a broken heart, or even something hopeful, like a small candle in the dark.

When you finish, take a moment to notice how sharing these feelings made you feel. Talking about grief, or drawing it, helps your heart feel a little lighter, like letting out a deep breath. Remember, there's no wrong way to feel — your grief is yours, and it matters.

Todays Date:

My Feelings Today

Circle how you're feeling right now (you can choose more than one):

Happy   Sad   Angry   Confused
Calm   Missing Mom   Loved

Then write or draw about your feelings below

Expressing My Feelings

Chapter 2 - My Memories

In this chapter, we will discover gentle ways to remember Mom.

You'll learn how drawing pictures, writing letters, and talking to people you trust can help you feel closer to her, even though she isn't here in the same way anymore. These activities are like little hugs for your heart. They remind you that Mom's love is still with you — in your memories, in your stories, and in all the ways she made you feel special.

Drawing my Memories

Sometimes, drawing can help us feel better. You can draw your favorite memory with Mom, like baking cookies or playing in the garden. Your drawings are like treasures that keep her close.

You can even make a special "Mom Memory Box." Fill it with drawings, photos, or small things that remind you of her. When you're sad, you can open it and remember all the love you shared.

Writing a Letter to Mom

Try writing a letter that starts with, "Dear Mom..." You can tell her about your day, your dreams, or how much you miss her.

Even though she can't write back, it can help your heart feel a little lighter.

Talking to a Trusted Adult

It's okay to say, "I miss Mom." Grown-ups won't always have the perfect answer, but they can listen and give you a big hug.

You can talk anytime you feel ready. Sharing memories or just sitting together can make things feel a little better.

Reflection 1

1. Write a letter to your Mom telling her how you feel today

Did you know that your heart has so much to say, and it can help to write it all down. You can start your letter however feels right for you, maybe with **"Dear Mom"** or **"Darling Mom."** There are no rules — this letter is just for you and her.

In your letter, you might want to tell Mom how you feel today. Are you feeling sad? Happy? Lonely? Brave? You can write, "I miss you so much today," or "I wish you were here to see my drawing," or even, "I felt your hug in the sunshine today."

You could also share something new you did — like a fun game you played, a yummy meal you ate, or a story you read. Maybe you want to tell her a secret, or ask her a question, or say how much you love her.

If you'd like, you can draw a little picture on your letter too. That picture is like a hug made of colors.

When you finish, you can fold up your letter and keep it somewhere safe, like a memory box, under your pillow, or even share it with someone you trust. Writing letters helps you feel close to Mom, like she is still listening with all her love.

Dear...........

1. **Write a letter to your Mom telling her how you feel today**

2. Sometimes your heart has so much to say, and it can help to write it all down. You can start your letter however feels right for you, maybe with **"Dear Mom"** or **"Darling Mom."** There are no rules — this letter is just for you and her.

3. In your letter, you might want to tell Mom how you feel today. Are you feeling sad? Happy? Lonely? Brave? You can write, "I miss you so much today," or "I wish you were here to see my drawing," or even, "I felt your hug in the sunshine today."

4. You could also share something new you did — like a fun game you played, a yummy meal you ate, or a story you read. Maybe you want to

tell her a secret, or ask her a question, or say how much you love her.

5. If you'd like, you can draw a little picture on your letter too. That picture is like a hug made of colors.

6. When you finish, you can fold up your letter and keep it somewhere safe, like a memory box, under your pillow, or even share it with someone you trust. Writing letters helps you feel close to Mom, like she is still listening with all her love.

Todays Date:

My Feelings Today

Circle how you're feeling right now (you can choose more than one):

Happy   Sad   Angry   Confused
Calm   Missing Mom   Loved

Then write or draw about your feelings below

A STAR IN MY HEART

Reflection 2

2. What are five colors that describe how you are feeling right now?

1.

2.

3.

4.

5.

What is the first color that you chose?

Why did you choose this color?

How are you feeling right now?

How does that color make you feel right now?

What is the second color that you chose?

Why did you choose this color?

How are you feeling right now?

How does that color make you feel?

What is the third color that you chose?

Why did you choose this color?

How are you feeling right now?

How does that color make you feel?

What is the fourth color that you chose?

Why did you choose this color?

How are you feeling right now?

How does that Color make you feel?

What is the fifth color that you chose?

Why did you choose this color?

How are you feeling right now?

How does that Color make you feel?

Todays Date:

My Feelings Today

Circle how you're feeling right now (you can choose more than one):

Happy   Sad   Angry   Confused
Calm   Missing Mom   Loved

Then write or draw about your feelings below

Reflection 3

3. Draw a heart and fill it with words or pictures that show your feelings

At times, feelings can be so big that it's hard to say them out loud. Drawing a heart is a simple and powerful way to hold those feelings in one special place. On a blank page, draw a big heart in the middle. Take your time — it can be any size, any color, and any shape you like.

Inside your heart, you can start adding words or little pictures. Think about how you're feeling today. Maybe you feel sad, brave, confused, or loved. You can write these words inside your heart.

Next, think about pictures that remind you of Mom or of happy memories. Maybe you want to draw a flower she liked, a star, a hug, or even something simple like her favorite color.

Your heart might have both happy and sad things inside, and that's perfectly okay. Grief can be a mix of sunshine and rain — both belong in your heart.

When you finish, look at all the feelings and memories you've placed there. That heart is yours to keep. You might hang it on your wall, tuck it in a memory box, or share it with someone who understands.

Your feelings matter, and putting them into this heart helps you remember that even when things feel hard, love is still inside you, shining bright.

Todays Date:

My Feelings Today

Circle how you're feeling right now (you can choose more than one):

Happy   Sad   Angry   Confused
Calm   Missing Mom   Loved

Then write or draw about your feelings below

Remembering Mom

Chapter 3

In this chapter, we will explore how to celebrate all the special Moments you shared with Mom.

You'll discover ways to remember her hugs, her smile, and her kindness. You'll also learn how to create a memory box, honor her with little traditions, and keep her love shining like a star in your heart. These ideas will help you feel close to Mom, showing you that even though she isn't here the same way, her love will always be part of you.

Special Moments Together

Think of a time Mom made you laugh or helped you when you were scared. These Moments are like stars that shine even on your darkest days.

Close your eyes and picture her voice, her hugs, and her smile. That love never fades. It's still blooming in your heart.

Creating a Memory Box

You can decorate a box and fill it with things that remind you of Mom. Maybe a photo, a note, or a small toy you shared.

You can add to it whenever you want. It's your special place to remember and feel connected.

Celebrating Her Life

Celebrating doesn't mean you're not sad. It means you're honoring how amazing she was.

You can plant flowers in her memory, bake her favorite cookies, or play a song she loved.

You could even create a special "Mom Day" where you do something she would have loved, just for her.

Reflection 1

1 What is one of your happiest memories with your Mom?

Take a moment and close your eyes. Think about a time when you and your Mom were together, and you felt really happy. Maybe you were baking cookies in the kitchen, reading a funny story before bed, playing outside in the sunshine, or even just cuddling on the couch. Picture that moment in your mind like a little movie playing just for you.

What did Mom say to you? How did her voice sound? What was the weather like that day? Try to remember the smells, the colors, and all the tiny details. Those small things can make your memory feel extra special.

Now, write down what happened, or draw a picture of it. You could even make a comic strip with speech bubbles to show what you and Mom were saying. If you'd like, share your happy memory with someone you trust, like a family member or a friend. Talking about good times can make your heart feel warm and remind you that Mom's love is still close.

Whenever you miss Mom, you can return to this happy memory and hold it in your heart like a spark of sunshine on a cloudy

day. Happy memories are like treasures
— they remind you that love never goes
away.

Todays Date:

My Feelings Today

Circle how you're feeling right now (you can choose more than one):

Happy   Sad   Angry   Confused
Calm   Missing Mom   Loved

Then write or draw about your feelings be-low

A STAR IN MY HEART

Todays Date:

My Feelings Today

Circle how you're feeling right now (you can choose more than one):

Happy   Sad   Angry   Confused
Calm   Missing Mom   Loved

Then write or draw about your feelings below

Reflection 2

2 Create a 'Memory Tree' — Each Leaf is a Memory of Your Mom

Let's make something beautiful to help you remember Mom — a Memory Tree! First, draw or paint a big, strong tree on a piece of paper. You can make its trunk as tall or as twisty as you like, and give it big branches reaching out in every direction. This tree is special because it will hold all the memories of your Mom that you want to keep safe.

Next, cut out lots of leaf shapes from colored paper, or draw them right onto your tree. On each leaf, write down a memory of your Mom. Maybe you remember the way she laughed, how she made your favorite dinner, or how her hugs made you feel calm and safe. You could also add memories like a trip you took together, a bedtime story, or the way she sang your name.

If you'd like, you can decorate each leaf with stickers, glitter, or even tiny drawings that remind you of her. Then, tape or glue each leaf to the branches of your tree. As you fill up the branches, you will see how many beautiful memories you have, all growing together like a forest of love.

Whenever you feel sad or miss your Mom, look at your Memory Tree. Touch each leaf and remember that every moment you wrote down is still alive in your heart. The Memory Tree is yours to keep, and you can always add more leaves whenever you think of new happy memories.

Todays Date:

My Feelings Today

Circle how you're feeling right now (you can choose more than one):

Happy   Sad   Angry   Confused
Calm   Missing Mom   Loved

Then write or draw about your feelings below

Reflection 3

3. Who Else Remembers Your Mom? Gather Their Stories!

At first, it can help your heart to hear how other people remember your Mom too. Think about who else loved her—maybe your grandparents, aunts, uncles, cousins, family friends, or neighbors. All of these people have their own special stories about your Mom, stories you might have never even heard before!

You can ask them questions like:

- What was Mom like when she was little?

- What is something funny or silly she did?

- What made her smile the most?

- Why did you love her?

When you sit down with them, you could use a notebook to write down what they share. Or you could record their voice on a phone with a grown-up's help, so you can listen again later. They might tell you about a time your Mom helped them, taught them something, or cheered them up when they were sad.

Each story is like a piece of a giant puzzle that shows how amazing your Mom was.

You might feel happy, surprised, or even a little sad hearing these stories—and that's all okay.

Once you collect the stories, you can write them in the space below or draw a picture to go with each one. This way, whenever you want to remember your Mom, you'll have not only your memories but also memories from the people who loved her too.

Every story you gather is another hug for your heart, reminding you that your Mom will always be remembered, not just by you but by everyone who cared about her.

Todays Date:

My Feelings Today

Circle how you're feeling right now (you can choose more than one):

Happy   Sad   Angry   Confused
Calm   Missing Mom   Loved

Then write or draw about your feelings below

The Journey of Grief

Chapter 4

In this chapter, we will learn about the journey of grief and what it really means.

Grief is a word for all the feelings your heart goes through when someone you love, like Mom, is no longer here. Sometimes those feelings can swirl around and feel heavy or confusing. That's okay. You'll discover that there is no right or wrong way to feel, and it's normal for emotions to come and go like waves. You'll also find out how doing familiar things — like playing, reading, or starting a small memory routine — can help you feel safe while you heal. Remember, this journey takes time, and you never have to walk it alone.

What Is Grief?

Grief is the name for all the feelings you have when someone you love is gone. It can feel like a mix of sadness, anger, love, and confusion. It's your heart learning how to hold on and let go at the same time.

Different Feelings Are Normal

You might feel okay one minute, then cry the next. You might feel nothing at all, then suddenly miss her a lot. All those feelings are part of grieving.

There's no right or wrong way to feel. However you feel—it's okay.

Finding Comfort in Routine

Doing your normal activities—like reading, drawing, or playing outside—can help. They remind your heart that you're still safe, and that life keeps going.

You can even make a new routine that includes remembering Mom. Like saying "Goodnight, Mom" before bed or writing in a journal each day.

Reflection 1

1 What kinds of feelings have you had since your Mom passed away?

Take a moment to think about all the different feelings you have had since your Mom died. Maybe you've felt sad, angry, confused, worried, or even peaceful for a moment. You might feel more than one feeling at once. That's okay! Write down or draw each feeling below, even if they seem mixed up. Naming your feelings helps your heart understand them better. You can also use colors to show your feelings, like blue for sadness or yellow for hope.

Todays Date:

My Feelings Today

Circle how you're feeling right now (you can choose more than one):

Happy   Sad   Angry   Confused
Calm   Missing Mom   Loved

Then write or draw about your feelings below

Reflection 2

2. Can you name a time when you felt both happy and sad at once?

Sometimes your heart can hold two feelings at the same time. Think about a moment when you were remembering your Mom — maybe it made you smile because it was such a warm memory, but then you felt tears come too. That's a normal part of grief. Write about that moment here. What made you feel happy? What made you feel sad? Think of it like a rainbow after a rain-storm — both sunshine and rain together.

Todays Date:

My Feelings Today

Circle how you're feeling right now (you can choose more than one):

Happy   Sad   Angry   Confused
Calm   Missing Mom   Loved

Then write or draw about your feelings be-

Reflection 3

3. Write about one way you've grown braver or stronger.

Since your Mom passed away, you have been doing something really brave — living each day with love and remembering her. Has there been a time you stood up for yourself, tried something new, or shared how you felt with someone you trust? That takes courage! Write about how you have grown braver or stronger, and how you think your Mom would be proud of you for that.

Todays Date:

My Feelings Today

Circle how you're feeling right now (you can choose moreMoman one):

Happy   Sad   Angry   Confused
Calm   Missing Mom   Loved

Then write or draw about your feelings below

Animal Friends and Their Stories

Chapter 5

In this chapter, we will meet some animal friends who also miss their Moms, just like you might.

Through their stories, you'll see how Tully the turtle, Laya the lioness, and Ollie the wise owl each find their own way to remember, feel close, and heal. These animal friends show us that love can stay with us, even after someone is gone, and that we can feel connected in our hearts no matter what. Their stories might help you feel braver, kinder to yourself, and remind you that you are never alone on your journey.

The Little Turtle's Goodbye

Tully the turtle missed his Mom so much that he hid deep inside his shell, hoping the world wouldn't notice how sad he felt. Every day felt hard without her hugs, and every night seemed a little colder without her voice to wish him sweet dreams. Sometimes, he wondered if his Mom could still see him, or if she knew how much he missed her. One evening, when the sky was sprinkled with stars, Tully bravely poked his head out and whispered, "Goodnight, Mama," to the night. A soft breeze touched his shell, and it felt like a hug from far away. From that night on, he talked to the stars every evening, telling them about his day, his hopes, and even his worries. Slowly, a tiny spark of peace grew in his heart, reminding him that love never really goes away — it just changes. When Tully closed his eyes, he imagined his Mom listening from the stars, proud of how he was trying to heal. That made his heart feel a little lighter, like carrying a lantern glowing softly through the night.

The Brave Lioness Remembers

Laya the lioness climbed the tall hill where she had once stood with her Mom, looking over the land together and feeling safe. Without her Mom, everything seemed quieter and lonelier, and her heart felt heavy with missing her Mom. Laya wanted to roar with all her sadness and anger, but instead, she let out a gentle, quiet roar filled with love and longing. The wind picked it up and carried it far across the grassy plains. As the breeze rushed past her, she felt something warm brush against her fur, almost like her mother's soft paw giving her courage. Laya closed her eyes and listened, imagining her mother's voice telling her to stay brave and strong. Every day after that, she climbed the hill to send her gentle roar into the wind, sharing her heart with her mother across the sky. When the wind answered with its soft whoosh, Laya smiled, knowing her mother's love was still out there, hugging her and helping her feel powerful, even when she was sad. That roar became her promise: to remember, to be strong, and to keep loving, no matter what.

The Wise Owl's Advice

Ollie the wise old owl perched high in the tallest tree, his feathers touched by the moonlight. One evening, a small bird landed on a nearby branch, tears filling her eyes. "I miss my Mom," the little bird whispered. Ollie nodded, understanding the ache in her heart. "When someone you love dies," he said gently, "their love doesn't leave you. It finds a new place to live — right here," and he tapped his feathered chest near his heart. The little bird looked confused, so Ollie explained, "Love is like a light. Even when you can't see it, it still shines and warms you." He told her that each time she remembered her Mom, that light grew brighter. "You might feel sad," Ollie added, "but that sadness means your love is strong." The bird listened closely, feeling a tiny bit of hope. Ollie encouraged her to talk to the stars, to sing her Mom's favorite song, and to tell stories about her. "All these things," he said, "help the love live on inside you." The little bird left with a lighter heart, carrying her Mom's love forward, just as Ollie promised she could, one beat at a time.

Reflection 1

1. Which animal story did you connect with the most? Why?

Think back to the stories about the turtle, the lioness, and the wise owl. Which one felt closest to your heart? Maybe you liked the turtle because he found comfort in the stars, or the lioness who roared out her love, or the owl who reminded you that love stays forever. Write about which animal friend you connected with most, and why it felt special to you

Todays Date:

My Feelings Today

Circle how you're feeling right now (you can choose more than one):

Happy   Sad   Angry   Confused
Calm   Missing Mom   Loved

Then write or draw about your feelings below

A STAR IN MY HEART

Reflection 2

2. Draw a picture of the animal that helped you feel better.

Now, use your imagination to draw the animal friend who helped you feel calm or brave. You could show them in their favorite place — like the turtle looking up at the stars, the lioness on her hill, or the owl sitting in a wise old tree. Add colors and details that make you happy. You might even add a little heart or star in the picture to show that they're helping you carry love forward.

Todays Date:

My Feelings Today

Circle how you're feeling right now (you can choose more than one):

Happy   Sad   Angry   Confused
Calm   Missing Mom   Loved

Then write or draw about your feelings below

Reflection 3

3. What advice would your animal friend give you today?

"Keep talking to the stars.""Your roar can be soft and full of love.""Your Mom's love will always stay with you."

If your animal friend could talk to you today, what kind words or advice would they give you? Maybe the turtle would say,

Maybe the lioness would remind you,

Or the owl might say,

Write down the advice your animal friend would give you, and read it whenever you feel lonely or scared. Their words can help guide your heart and give you courage.

Todays Date:

My Feelings Today

Circle how you're feeling right now (you can choose more than one):

Happy   Sad   Angry   Confused

Calm   Missing Mom   Loved

Then write or draw about your feelings be-

Activities for Healing

Chapter 6

In this chapter, we will explore some caring and creative activities that can help you feel a little better when you miss Mom. Grief can feel heavy, like carrying a giant backpack on your shoulders, but doing gentle things with your hands, heart, and imagination can make it lighter. These activities will give you a way to share your feelings, remember happy Moments, and hold on to the love you still have for Mom. Whether you choose to write, make something with your hands, or walk in nature, you'll find ways to bring comfort to your heart. You don't have to rush or do every-thing at once — just take your time and do what feels good for you. These ideas are here to help you heal, one small step at a time. Let's discover them together, and know that every memory and every feeling is welcome here.

Grief Journaling for Kids

Keeping a grief journal can be like having a quiet friend who is always ready to lis-ten. When you write in your journal, you make a special space where your heart can let out all the feelings it is holding. You might begin with simple words like, "Today I remembered..." or "Dear Mom, I wish you could see..." and let your thoughts flow. Maybe you want to write about something that happened at school, a dream you had, or a silly memory you shared with Mom. Nothing has to be perfect in your journal — your spelling, handwriting, or even the way you arrange your words doesn't matter at all. You might want to add drawings, poems, song lyrics, or little photos that remind you of Mom. Some kids like to decorate their journal with stickers, washi tape, or pressed flowers, making it feel like a treasure book full of love. Writing can help you feel lighter inside, like letting your heart take a deep breath. If you ever feel like you miss Mom so much it hurts, you can return to your journal and talk to her there. It's a safe place, a space where your memories and feelings can stay close, waiting to comfort you whenever you need them.

Fun Crafts to Remember Mom

Using your hands to make something beautiful can feel a lot like giving your heart a hug. You might start by creating a colorful handprint heart, dipping your hands in paint and pressing them onto paper to form a heart shape. Inside, you could write something kind about Mom or even a short note to her. Another craft idea is to make a picture frame from cardboard — you can cut out shapes, color them, add sparkly stickers, beads, or ribbon, and place a photo of Mom in the middle. Each time you look at it, you will see her smiling back at you. You could also make a rainbow collage with colored paper or fabric. Each color might remind you of a feeling or memory: red for warm hugs, yellow for her bright laugh, green for her love of the outdoors, blue for peaceful Moments, and purple for her kindness. These crafts are more than decorations — they are love you can see and touch. Every time you walk by them, they will remind you that Mom's love is still all around you. And if you'd like, you can make more than one to give to other family members, sharing the love and keeping her memory alive together.

Nature Walks to Reflect

Going for a nature walk can feel like taking a calm, gentle journey where you let your heart rest. Walking outside helps you breathe more deeply, and you can feel the breeze on your face, hear the rustle of leaves, and listen to birds singing their songs. While you walk, you might see something that reminds you of Mom — a flower she liked, the color of the sky, or even a butterfly fluttering past. If you spot something that makes you think of her, you can pick it up and save it, like a shiny rock, a soft feather, or a tiny flower. When you bring it home, you might place it somewhere special, like next to her picture or in a memory box. You could even start a "Mom collection" of nature treasures, adding to it each time you walk. Being in nature helps us remember that life changes with the seasons, but love stays. Even if Mom isn't here the way she used to be, the wind, the sun, and the world around you can help you feel connected to her. You might want to talk to her while you walk, sharing your thoughts or telling her what you see. These peaceful walks can be a kind of secret visit, where your heart gets to talk to Mom and remember she is still with you in spirit, every step of the way.

Reflection 1

1. Make a simple plan: What can you do this week to feel a little better?

Sometimes making a gentle plan can help you feel more steady. Take a Moment to think about what might help your heart this week. You could write down one small thing for each day. For example:

- Monday: Draw a picture of Mom and color it with happy colors.(Draw it below)

- Tuesday: Read a favorite story that she used to read to you.

What story did you read? Write about it in the space below

- Wednesday: Go outside and look for something beautiful in nature, like a flower or a butterfly.

Where in nature did you go?

What did you see?

- Thursday: Bake or help cook something that reminds you of Mom.

What did you bake or cook? Write or draw about it below

- Friday: Talk to someone you trust about a memory you miss.
  You can make up your own plan, too! Maybe you want to listen to a song she liked, light a candle, or cuddle up with your favorite blanket. You can even decorate your plan with stickers or colors to make it feel like

ate your plan with stickers or colors to make it feel like a little promise to yourself. Remember, you don't have to do everything perfectly. Even one tiny act of love can help your heart feel braver this week.

Who did you talk too?

What do you do to help your hert feel braver? Write or draw about it below.

Todays Date:

My Feelings Today

Circle how you're feeling right now (you can choose more than one):

Happy   Sad   Angry   Confused
Calm   Missing Mom   Loved

Then write or draw about your feelings below

Reflection 2

2. Try a craft or activity

Crafts can be like magic for your heart. Think about something you might enjoy making, like a memory bracelet with beads in Mom's favorite colors, or a drawing of your family with Mom's smiling face in it. Maybe you'd like to fold a paper heart and write a secret message to her inside. You could also build a small fairy house or nature sculpture outside and dedicate it to Mom, imagining she'd love to see it.

After you finish your craft, take a quiet Moment to notice how it makes you feel. Does it bring you a warm feeling, like a hug? Do you feel a bit sad but also proud? It's okay to feel both! You could write down what you made and how it felt, for example: "I made a rainbow drawing for Mom. It made me feel happy and a little teary at the same time." Your crafts and creations are ways to keep love alive, one beautiful piece at a time.

What did you make?

How did it make you feel?

Todays Date:

My Feelings Today

Circle how you're feeling right now (you can choose more than one):

Happy   Sad   Angry   Confused
Calm   Missing Mom   Loved

Then write or draw about your feelings below

Reflection 3

3. Write or draw what you saw on your last nature walk.

"On my nature walk, I noticed...""This pink flower reminded me of the ones Mom planted in our garden."

Think back to your last nature walk — what did you see, hear, and feel? Maybe there were flowers blooming, birds singing, or the leaves dancing in the wind. Did you see a butterfly, or a ladybug crawling on a leaf?

Take a piece of paper and write about it, starting with,

Or draw a picture with all the details — the shape of the clouds, the color of the sky, the sound of the breeze. You might even want to add something about Mom, like,

If you'd like, collect a small treasure on your next walk, like a smooth stone or a shiny leaf, and tape it onto your page. Nature can feel like a quiet friend that listens to you, reminding you that life keeps going and love never fades. Your drawing or writing can become a memory all its own, something to return to whenever you want to feel calm or connected.

Todays Date:

My Feelings Today

Circle how you're feeling right now (you can choose more than one):

Happy   Sad   Angry   Confused
Calm   Missing Mom   Loved

Then write or draw about your feelings below

Talking About Death

Chapter 7

In this chapter, we will explore how to talk about something really hard: what it means when someone dies. It can feel scary or confusing to hear the word "death," especially when it is about your Mom. You might have lots of questions and wonder if it is okay to ask them. Guess what? It is. There is no wrong way to talk about what happened, and there is no wrong time to bring up your feelings. In this chapter, you will discover simple, honest words to help you understand, learn how to ask the questions swirling in your mind, and find out that it's perfectly fine to talk when you feel ready. Talking about death might feel painful, but it can also help you feel less afraid and more connected to the people who love you. Let's walk through this together, one gentle step at a time.

Simple Words to Explain

Sometimes grown-ups use words that maybe a little confusing, like "passed away" or "gone to a better place." That can make things even harder to understand. It's okay to use simple words: **Mom died.** That means her body stopped working, and she can't come back. Her heart stopped beating, and her breath stopped moving in and out. It doesn't mean you did something wrong, or that she stopped loving you. It doesn't mean she didn't want to stay. It just means that her body couldn't work anymore, and death is something that happens to all living things, even though it feels unfair and really sad.

Even if her body isn't here, Mom's love is. Every hug she gave, every song she sang, every bedtime story she read — those things are still alive in your memories. Love is bigger than a body, and it doesn't end. When you talk about her, draw about her, or remember something she taught you, you are keeping her love shining in your heart.

If you want, you can say it in your own way: "My Mom died, but I still love her." Saying the words might feel like a giant storm at first, but the more you say them, the easier it becomes to hold onto the truth that her love is still yours forever. It's okay to ask a grown-up to help you find the words, too. They can sit with you and explain again if you need. Remember, there are no silly questions, and there is no shame in wanting to understand. Talking about death with simple, gentle words can make your heart feel lighter, even if it feels hard at first.

Questions You Might Ask

When someone we love dies, so many questions pop up in our heads, like popcorn popping in a pan. You might wonder, "Where is she now? Does she still see me? Why did this happen? Will I forget her?" All of these questions are normal and brave. Sometimes, grown-ups don't have perfect answers, but they will still try to help you feel safe.

Maybe someone will say Mom is in heaven, or in the stars, or watching over you like a guardian angel. Some people believe that the soul goes to a special place full of peace, while others believe the love stays right here in your heart. It's okay to believe what feels right for you, and it's okay if you change your mind later.

You might also worry about forgetting her. That's normal, too. But the truth is, love leaves deep marks on our hearts — the kind you don't ever lose. Even if you can't remember every single thing about your Mom, the feeling of her love will always be there, like a warm spark inside.

If you have a question, you can write it down or ask someone you trust, like a parent, grandparent, teacher, or counselor. They might not have all the answers, but they can listen to your worries and help you feel less alone. If you'd rather, you can even draw your questions in a notebook or talk to Mom out loud, saying, "I wonder where you are now, Mom." That's brave and kind.

Remember, wondering about death does not mean something is wrong with you. It means you are trying to understand something really big. That is strong. That is loving. And it shows how much you care.

Finding the Right Time to Talk

Some people think there is only one "right" time to talk about hard things, but really, you get to choose when you feel ready. Maybe you want to talk about Mom at bedtime, when you feel safe under the covers. Maybe you feel like sharing memories on a walk outside or while you're coloring at the kitchen table. Some kids like to talk in the car with their grown-up because it feels calm and quiet.

You can talk any time a memory pops up, or a question sneaks into your mind. You don't have to wait until someone asks you how you're feeling. You can start the con-versation with, "Can we talk about Mom?" or "I'm wondering about what happened." Grown-ups might not always have perfect words, but most of them will listen with their hearts open, ready to help.

If you're scared to talk, you can try writing your feelings down first, or drawing a pic-ture of what you want to say. Then you can share the drawing or words with a trusted person to help you get started. It's also okay to talk and cry at the same time, or even talk and laugh — memories can make us feel both.

Remember, your heart is the boss of when you're ready. It might take days, weeks, or months before you want to say certain things. That's okay. There is no timer on grief. There is no "too late" to talk. Every time you share a piece of your heart, you are taking a brave step toward healing. And you don't have to do it alone — there are people who will walk with you, every single step of the way.

Reflection 1

1. What Is One Question You Still Have About Death?

Death can be confusing, even for grown-ups. You might still have big questions in your mind, like: "Where did Mom go?" or "Why can't I see her again?" or "Is she watching over me?" These questions are brave and important.

Try to think of **one question** that feels the biggest in your heart right now. Write it down on a piece of paper, or say it out loud to someone you trust. Maybe it sounds like: "Why did Mom have to die?" or "Can she hear me when I talk to her?"

You can decorate the page with little drawings or colors that help you feel calm while you think. Remember, no question is too silly or wrong. Grown-ups may not always have every answer, but they can help you explore what feels true and comforting for you.

If you'd like, you can make a "question box," where you drop in all your wondering thoughts as they come. Then, when you feel ready, you can take one out and talk about it. It might feel scary at first, but asking your question can help you feel lighter and remind you that you don't have to carry these worries alone.

Todays Date:

My Feelings Today

Circle how you're feeling right now (you can choose more than one):

Happy   Sad   Angry   Confused
Calm   Missing Mom   Loved

Then write or draw about your feelings be-

Reflection 2

2. Who Can You Talk To When You're Feeling Sad or Confused?

Sometimes grief feels so heavy it makes you want to hide. But you don't have to go through those big feelings alone. Take a Moment to make a list of the people you trust who you could talk to. Maybe it's Dad, a grandparent, a teacher, your best friend, or even a counselor at school.

Write down their names, or draw a picture of them. Next to each name, you could add something like, "They give good hugs," or "They listen to me," or "They make me feel safe."

If you want, you can hang this list in your room or keep it in your backpack, so whenever you feel sad or confused, you can look at it and remember: "I am not alone."

It's also okay to change who you talk to, depending on how you feel. Some days you might want to be with family, other days with a friend, and sometimes you might even want to talk to a kind grown-up you haven't talked to before. That's perfectly okay.

Remember, sharing your heart is a brave and strong thing to do, and there are people who want to help you carry your heavy feelings.

Todays Date:

My Feelings Today

Circle how you're feeling right now (you can choose more than one):

Happy   Sad   Angry   Confused
Calm   Missing Mom   Loved

Then write or draw about your feelings below

Reflection 3

3. Create a List of 'Feelings Words' That You Can Use When Talking to Others

Sometimes it's hard to explain how you feel, because grief can make your emotions swirl around like a storm. Making a feelings-word list can help you share what's in your heart.

First, think of some words for **sad** feelings. You might write:

- Lonely

- Heartbroken

- Lost

- Upset

- Missing someone

Then, think of words for **angry** feelings, like:

- Mad

- Frustrated

- Annoyed

- Jealous

- Scared

Next, write down words for **hopeful or peaceful** feelings, such as:

- Calm

- Brave

- Safe

- Loved

- Proud

Decorate your word list with colors or small doodles if you like. Maybe blue means calm, yellow means hopeful, and gray means sad.

Whenever you feel stuck or confused, you can look at this list and point to the word that matches how your heart feels. You can even say, "Today I feel lonely," or "I feel a little hopeful," so that others can understand and help you.

Feelings change all the time, and that's normal. This word list is like a secret code to help you talk about them. Each time you use these words, you are being honest and brave — and that helps your heart heal.

You can list the words below

Todays Date:

My Feelings Today

Circle how you're feeling right now (you can choose more than one):

Happy   Sad   Angry   Confused
Calm   Missing Mom   Loved

Then write or draw about your feelings below

150

Cultural Perspectives on Grief

Chapter 8

In this chapter, we're going to travel around the world through stories and traditions. Every culture has its own way of remembering people who have died, like lighting candles, sharing favorite foods, or dancing to music. These traditions help keep love alive. Sometimes, hearing how other people honor their loved ones can give us ideas for remembering ours, too. You might even want to create your own special way to think of your mom. In this chapter, you'll discover how people everywhere turn grief into something beautiful — and how you can, too.

How Different Cultures Remember

All around the world, people have found meaningful ways to remember the people they love. These traditions help carry stories forward and keep connections strong, even after someone has died. In some places, families gather together to light candles and say prayers, sending messages of love into the night. In other places, people wear special clothes, like bright colors, to show that they are celebrating a life rather than only being sad. Some people sing songs that their ancestors sang long ago, letting those words wrap around them like a warm hug.

For example, in Japan, many families visit their loved ones' graves during Obon, a special festival that includes lanterns and dances. In parts of Africa, families might drum and sing for days, believing the rhythms help guide a loved one's spirit. In New Zealand, Māori communities hold tangihanga, where whānau (family) come together on the marae to cry, laugh, sing, and remember.

Every tradition has its own way of saying: You mattered. You are still loved.

Learning about these different customs reminds us that no one grieves alone. Even though people might live far away from us, their hearts feel something similar. These traditions show that love is a language everyone understands, no matter where they come from.

Stories from Around the World

Stories travel, just like people do, and they carry love and memories with them. In Mexico, there is a beautiful tradition called **Día de los Muertos** — Day of the Dead. Families build colorful altars covered in flowers, photos, and even food their loved ones enjoyed. They believe their loved ones come back to visit during this time, so it is a celebration of life and memory, not just sadness.

In Ireland, there is a tradition of telling stories and singing songs at a wake, often through the night. People gather around to share funny memories, cry together, and comfort one another. These stories remind everyone that the person who died left behind love and laughter.

In Aotearoa (New Zealand), Māori tangihanga ceremonies can last for several days. Family and community members come together, sleeping on the marae, sharing stories, songs, and food while remembering the person who has died. There is time for crying, for celebrating, and for speaking directly to the person who has passed on.

Every one of these traditions teaches us that remembering someone isn't only about feeling sad. It can also be about celebrating the good times, sharing stories, and building new memories around those we've lost. When we hear stories from other places, it can spark ideas for our own ways to remember our Moms. Maybe you'll decide to draw a picture each year, light a candle, or sing a favorite song. Traditions come from stories, and you can help create your own, too.

Learning from Others' Experiences

When you learn about how people in other cultures cope with grief, it can feel like your heart is holding hands with theirs. You realize that grief is part of being human, and people everywhere try to find ways to hold on to love. You might learn from a friend that their family lights incense or leaves food for their ancestors. Or someone else might share that they pray in a special place, or write letters to the person who died.

Knowing these traditions can give you ideas for your own family. You might think, "Maybe I could start a Mom Day, where we do something she loved." Or "I want to light a candle every year on her birthday." These acts help your love stay bright, just like families in other parts of the world.

When you hear about how others find strength, it can remind you that you're not alone. Even if your grief feels heavy, there are people all over the world carrying their own heavy hearts, too. Together, you are part of a huge family of people who love deeply.

That's why talking to others about their experiences is so important. It helps you see that grief changes over time, and that it is okay to smile, laugh, and celebrate while remembering. You can borrow ideas from other cultures or make your own, mixing them together like a beautiful rainbow of remembrance. However you choose to remember, know that your way is the right way, and it honors the love that will always live in your heart.

Reflection 1

1 What is something new you learned about how other cultures remember loved ones?

Different cultures around the world have unique and beautiful ways of honoring people who have died. Maybe you learned about Día de los Muertos in Mexico, where families decorate colorful altars with flowers and favorite foods to remember their loved ones. Or perhaps you discovered how in Japan, people send floating lanterns down rivers to guide their ancestors' spirits. Some people in Aotearoa (New Zealand) hold long tangihanga gatherings with storytelling and singing to celebrate someone's life.

Think about one of these traditions that stood out to you. What made it feel special? Was it the way people gather together, the bright decorations, or the songs and prayers? Why do you think these customs might help people feel closer to someone they have lost?

In the space below, write about the cultural tradition you found most interesting. You can even draw a picture of what you imagine it looks like! If you could try one of these customs with your own family, what would you choose and why?

Remember, there is no one "right" way to remember someone you love. Exploring how others do it around the world might give you ideas for your own way of celebrating your mom's memory. Write or draw what you learned, and think about how it makes you feel knowing that love is honored in so many beautiful ways across the globe.

Todays Date:

My Feelings Today

Circle how you're feeling right now (you can choose more than one):

Happy   Sad   Angry   Confused
Calm   Missing Mom   Loved

Then write or draw about your feelings below

Reflection 2

2. Write about a new tradition or goal that helps you remember your Mom with love.

Creating new traditions can be a comforting way to keep your Mom close to your heart. Maybe you'd like to start a "Mom's Day" each year, where you do something she loved—like baking cookies, reading a favorite story, or planting flowers.

Or maybe you could set a goal, like learning a new skill or being extra kind to others, because you know your Mom would be proud of you. You might decide to write her a letter every year on her birthday, telling her about all the things you have done and how much you still love her.

Write down your new tradition or goal in a journal. Describe why you chose it, what makes it special, and how it makes you feel. You could even draw a picture of what this tradition might look like.

When you do these things, it can feel like sharing a piece of your heart with your Mom. These loving traditions or goals help you carry her forward, making sure her love is still a part of your life, even as you grow.

Todays Date:

My Feelings Today

166

Circle how you're feeling right now (you can choose more than one):

Happy   Sad   Angry   Confused
Calm   Missing Mom   Loved

Then write or draw about your feelings below

Reflection 3

3. Design a 'Remembrance Day' activity for your family or class.

Pretend you are planning a day just for re-membering people we love who have died. What would you do on that day? Would you sing songs, paint pictures, or share a big meal? Make a list or draw a schedule of the day. Think about decorations, foods, and what you'd like to say or do. Designing a day like this can help you feel proud to share stories and keep memories alive.

Todays Date:

My Feelings Today

Circle how you're feeling right now (you can choose more than one):

Happy   Sad   Angry   Confused
Calm   Missing Mom   Loved

Then write or draw about your feelings below

Moving Forward Together

Chapter 9

In this chapter, we're going to think about how to keep moving forward after losing someone so special, like your mom. It might feel scary to take steps into the future without her, but you don't have to leave her behind. Her love is always with you, wrapped around your heart. We'll talk about how to find joy again, how to make new traditions to remember her, and how to look ahead with hope. Even on days when you feel sad, her spark can guide you, helping you feel strong and loved every step of the way.

Finding Joy After Sadness

After someone we love dies, like our mom, it can feel like the world will never be happy again. You might think laughing means you're forgetting her, but that's not true at all. Joy and sadness can live side by side in your heart. When you feel happy again—like laughing with a friend or playing your favorite game—that doesn't mean you have stopped loving Mom. It just means you are carrying her love with you into today.

Think of joy as a way to honor her. Maybe your mom loved to see you smile. If you laugh again, you're letting her love keep working through you. Remember, it is perfectly okay to feel good sometimes, even after a really big loss. Happiness is like sunshine on a cloudy day—it can peek through the sadness and help you grow stronger.

You might try to notice tiny joyful things, like a bird singing, a rainbow after rain, or the warm feeling of a cozy blanket. Those small moments can help you remember that life still holds goodness, even if you miss your mom. It's brave to find hope again, and it shows how strong your heart really is. Joy will never erase the love you have for your mom; it will simply give that love new places to shine.

New Traditions to Honor Mom

When someone dies, we can feel afraid that we'll forget them or that their memory will fade. But you can create new ways to keep their love close. These are called traditions, and they help you feel connected. For example, you could start a "Mom's Day" every year, where you do something she loved—like baking her favorite cookies, reading her favorite book, or going to a place you visited together.

You could also make a small space in your room just for her. Place a photo there, or something that belonged to her, like a scarf or a necklace. Whenever you miss her, you can visit that space and feel comforted. These small rituals become an-chors that help you feel safe and connect-ed.

Another idea is to make a craft in her hon-or, like a painting or a memory jar. You might put in little notes about your favorite times with her, or decorate it with colors that remind you of her. These traditions don't have to be fancy—they just need to come from your heart.

By honoring your mom in these ways, you are keeping her love alive, like a candle that never goes out. Traditions can help you share your memories with friends or family, making sure everyone remembers how amazing she was. They help you move forward while still carrying her with you, and that is a beautiful way to heal.

Reflection 1

1. What gives you hope when you feel really sad?

When you feel really sad and miss your Mom, it can help to think about what brings you hope. Hope is like a tiny light that shines even in a dark room. Maybe you feel hopeful when you remember that your mom wanted you to be happy, or when you think of a fun memory that makes you smile. Maybe seeing your family together, hugging a pet, or talking to a friend gives you hope.

Draw or write about those things that help you feel stronger on the hard days. You could even make a "hope list" with things that cheer you up: warm sunshine, a rainbow, a favorite story, or a friend who listens. Keep the list somewhere safe so you can look at it whenever you need to feel a bit braver.

If you want, you can also draw a symbol of hope, like a flower growing or a candle burning brightly, to remind you that sadness doesn't last forever. Hope is always there, ready to help you heal. Whenever you feel that gentle spark of hope, know that your Mom would be proud of how strong you are becoming.

Todays Date:

My Feelings Today

Circle how you're feeling right now (you can choose more than one):

Happy   Sad   Angry   Confused
Calm   Missing Mom   Loved

Then write or draw about your feelings below

Reflection 2

3. How have you changed or grown since your loss?

After losing someone as special as your mom, you might notice you've changed. Maybe you feel more caring toward others, or more understanding when someone is sad. Perhaps you've learned to be braver, or you've found new ways to talk about your feelings.

Take a moment to think about the ways you have grown. Write them down or draw pictures to show what feels different about you now. You might say, "I'm stronger because I can talk about missing Mom," or "I learned how to help a friend who feels sad."

Sometimes, grief can help you notice just how big your heart really is. Even though you still hurt, you may see how you've become more patient, kinder, or more thankful for happy moments.

Write about the things you're proud of, no matter how small. You can share them with someone you trust, like a parent or teacher, so they can celebrate your bravery too. Your mom's love is still inside you, helping you grow in amazing ways, one day at a time.

MICHELLE HUIRAMA

Todays Date:

My Feelings Today

Circle how you're feeling right now (you can choose more than one):

Happy   Sad   Angry   Confused
Calm   Missing Mom   Loved

Then write or draw about your feelings below

Support for Parents

Chapter 10

This chapter is for grown-ups who want to help kids after someone very important has died — like Mom. Children look to the caring adults around them to feel safe, loved, and supported, even when life feels upside down. In this chapter, we'll explore gentle ways to talk with kids, to answer their brave questions, and to create spaces where big feelings can be shared. You don't have to have perfect answers — just showing up with an open heart is enough. These ideas will help you guide your child with honesty, compassion, and hope, one conversation and one memory at a time.

Helping Your Child Grieve

Children may have so many questions when someone dies, and those questions might come up again and again as they grow. Try to answer simply and truthfully. You can say, "Mom died, which means her body stopped working, and she can't come back." That may feel hard to say, but children trust clear, gentle words much more than silence or confusing phrases.

It's also important to let kids share their feelings, no matter how messy those feelings might be. Some days, they might be angry. Other days, they might cry or even laugh about a funny memory and feel confused. That's all normal. You can remind them: "All feelings are okay. You don't have to hide anything from me."

Make sure you give children enough time to process. Avoid saying things like "You should be over it by now." Instead, help them see grief as a journey, not a race. Sitting with them during hard moments and simply listening is one of the most healing gifts you can offer.

Also, model your own healthy grief. If you feel sad, it's okay to say so. Children learn that if grown-ups can talk about grief, they can too. Let them see you remember good things, shed tears, and still keep moving forward with love. That honesty gives them courage to share, and helps them know that even though things will never be the same, you will face this loss together.

Finding Support Groups

You don't have to do this alone, and neither does your child. There are many support options made just for grieving kids. Look for programs through local hospices, churches, mental health centers, or children's hospitals. Many of these programs use art, play, and stories to help kids explore loss in a safe place.

Support groups let kids meet other children who have lost a parent. This can be powerful because it shows them they are not alone — other kids understand how heavy grief feels. When kids hear each other's stories, they may feel braver to tell their own. That sense of community and belonging is an incredible comfort.

If a group isn't available, consider working with a counselor or therapist who is trained in child grief. One-on-one sessions can help your child express feelings they might hold back at home.

Books, too, can be healing. Children's grief stories can spark good conversations and help kids feel seen. Your local librarian, school counselor, or pediatrician might have suggestions about age-appropriate books that show hope and honesty.

Even small community rituals, like candlelight ceremonies or memory walls, can help children honor their lost parent. Ask your child if they'd like to participate — or just to watch. Let them know there is no right or wrong way to grieve, and there is no deadline for feeling better.

When children feel supported not only by you, but also by a wider community, they grow stronger and more confident that they can survive this loss, and keep carrying love forward.

Encouraging Emotional Expression

Children are full of feelings — and grief can make those feelings seem even bigger. Encouraging your child to express emotions in healthy ways is one of the best gifts you can give.

You can start by giving them a journal and saying, "This is a safe place for any feelings you want to put down." Suggest drawing, coloring, or writing letters to their Mom whenever they want to. Art can be a gentle way to express what words sometimes can't say.

Storytelling is another powerful tool. You might invite your child to tell stories about Mom at dinner, before bed, or during a family gathering. Let them share silly memories, warm memories, even sad memories — it all helps them feel connected.

Rituals can also bring comfort. Maybe each night, you light a candle together and say one thing you love about Mom. Or you plant flowers in her honor. These rituals help kids feel rooted, like they have a path through grief.

It's important to revisit memories often. Sometimes grown-ups worry this will make kids sad, but children usually find relief in talking about the person they miss. When you talk about Mom, you show that re-membering is allowed, and love doesn't have to disappear.

Let your child see you honor memories, too. If you cry, say, "I'm sad today because I miss Mom." That gives kids permission to feel all their feelings without shame. Re-mind them that grief doesn't have to be "fixed" or pushed away — it needs to be heard, and you are there to listen, as many times as it takes.

Reflection 1

1 What do you wish grown-ups knew about how kids feel grief?

Think about the things you wish adults understood. Maybe you wish they knew that you sometimes cry at school, or that you feel okay one minute and sad the next. Maybe you want them to know you like to talk about Mom, even if you also feel tears. Write down or draw those wishes. You could make a letter that says, "Dear grown-ups, please remember..." and list what you want them to know about your heart. Sharing this can help the adults in your life support you even better.

Todays Date:

My Feelings Today

Circle how you're feeling right now (you can choose more than one):

Happy   Sad   Angry   Confused
Calm   Missing Mom   Loved

Then write or draw about your feelings below

Reflection 2

.2. Draw or write how a trusted adult helps you feel safe.

Think of someone in your life who makes you feel calm and cared for — it could be your dad, grandma, auntie, teacher, counselor, or another grown-up you trust. What do they do that helps you feel better when you are sad, scared, or confused? Maybe they give you a warm hug, listen to your worries without interrupting, or sit quietly with you until you feel more peaceful.

In the space below, you can draw a picture of this trusted adult helping you. Maybe you draw them giving you a hug, reading you a story, or holding your hand. You could also write about how they help you. Do they remind you of happy memories? Do they help you talk about your mom?

Try to include details about what makes you feel safe with them. Is it their gentle voice? Their kind eyes? The way they never rush you? Writing or drawing about these moments can remind you that you are not alone, and there are people around you who will always look out for you.

Todays Date:

My Feelings Today

Circle how you're feeling right now (you can choose more than one):

Happy   Sad   Angry   Confused
Calm   Missing Mom   Loved

Then write or draw about your feelings below

Reflection 3

3. What is one thing you want to share with your family about your feelings?

Sometimes it can feel hard to tell your family how you're really feeling inside, especially after your mom has died. You might worry about making them sad, or think they won't understand. But sharing your heart can help everyone feel closer and less alone.

Think about something you wish your family could know. It could be as simple as,

"I miss Mom a lot," or "Sometimes I still feel really sad." Maybe you want them to know that remembering happy memories makes you smile, or that certain days (like birthdays or holidays) feel extra hard for you.

In the space below, write about one feeling you want to share. You can also draw a picture that shows this feeling if it feels easier. Being honest with your family helps them support you better, and it helps you feel stronger and braver, too. Remember — your feelings matter, and the people who love you want to hear them.

Todays Date:

My Feelings Today

Circle how you're feeling right now (you can choose more than one):

Happy   Sad   Angry   Confused
Calm   Missing Mom   Loved

Then write or draw about your feelings below

Grown-Up Reflections

Supporting Grieving Children

Listen More Than You Speak

Children often express grief in small, scattered ways. Be patient and let them talk when they're ready—without pushing for answers or fixing every silence. Simply being present matters more than saying the "right" thing.

Watch for Changes in Behavior

Grieving kids may become quieter, more emotional, or act out in unexpected ways. Gentle routines, extra patience, and comfort through play or art can help them feel safe again.

Create Opportunities to Remember

Encourage memory-making activities like drawing, storytelling, or visiting a special place. These help children process their loss while feeling connected to the person they miss.

Support, Don't Rush

There's no timeline for grief. Some days they may laugh, other days they may cry—and both are normal. Let them go at their own pace, and reassure them that their feelings are okay.

Take Care of Yourself, Too

Children often mirror the emotions of the adults around them. If you are also grieving, showing how you gently manage your own sadness can help model healthy coping for them. It's okay to say, "I feel sad too, but we'll get through this together."

A Note for Grown-Ups

Dear Caring Grown-Up,

Thank you for sharing A Star in My Heart with your child. Grief is a deeply personal journey, especially for children who might not yet have the words for such big, confusing feelings. This book was created to offer a safe, gentle, and comforting way to help your child explore what it means to lose their Mom, while also celebrating the love that will always stay with them.

If you can, encourage your child to talk about their mother — to share memories, stories, and even the hard or scary questions. Listen with an open heart, without trying to "fix" their feelings, and remind them that every emotion is okay. Reading these chapters together, revisiting them, or trying out the activities can open the door to conversations that help your child heal and feel stronger over time.

Grief does not follow a schedule. Some days will feel harder, and some days lighter, and it is perfectly okay for your child to move through those waves at their own pace. Be patient, and remind them as often as you can that they are never alone.

May the love you remember, the memories you celebrate, and the hope you build together bring gentle comfort and healing to both of your hearts.

With warmth and understanding,

Michelle Huirama

Final Reflection

You've made it through this book, and that's something to be proud of.

Losing your Mom may always leave a space in your heart—but her love, her stories, and everything she taught you… those things stay.

Whenever you miss her, remember: it's okay to feel all your feelings. It's okay to cry. It's okay to smile again.

You carry her with you—in your thoughts, your dreams, and your kindness.

She is your forever star.

And your heart?

It still glows.

Let's Meet Michelle Huirama

Hi, I'm Michelle—a children's author who writes with heart, hope, and healing in mind.

I created A Star in My Heart to support kids who are learning to live without their Mom. After facing my own loss, I realized how powerful stories can be in helping children understand grief, process emotions, and find comfort in the love that never truly disappears.

This book is filled with warmth, honesty, and gentle guidance—because every child deserves to know that even though their Mom is gone, her love is still with them... lighting the way forward, one memory at a time.

Ko Tukotuku te Reikura

Ko Tamainupo te Hapu

Ko Karioi te Maunga

Ko Waikato te Ipukarea

Ko Tainui te Waka

With Love

Written with empathy and care,

this story reminds families that saying goodbye doesn't mean forgetting.

It means remembering with love.

And whenever you're ready, you can come back to these pages,

draw another picture, write a new memory, or just sit and remember.

Your love for your Mother never ends, and this book will always be here for you.

With love,

Michelle

A Healing Grief Series

For children aged 7 and up

Grief is the shape love takes when someone we care about is no longer here.

Love That Stays is a heartfelt book series designed to support older children as they navigate the complex emotions that come with loss. Whether it's a grandparent, parent, sibling, friend, or pet—these books gently walk with kids through the waves of grief, offering tools to help them remember, reflect, and begin to heal.

With compassionate language, thoughtful chapters, and creative activities like journaling, storytelling, memory-making, and mindfulness, each book invites children to explore their emotions at their own pace. These stories honor the unbreakable bond between kids and the people they love—showing that even though someone may be gone, the love they shared will always remain.

Love That Stays reminds young readers that grief is not about forgetting—it's about remembering, growing, and carrying love forward, one page at a time.

Remember

Grief isn't something we "get over." It's something we learn to carry—with time, love, and support.

Remember:

You are not alone.

Your Mom's love didn't end—it just changed shape.

It lives on in your memories, your smile, and the way you move through the world.

You're part of a story filled with love, and your heart is still writing it—one day at a time.

You're doing so well. Keep going!

www.ingramcontent.com/pod-product-compliance
Lightning Source LLC
LaVergne TN
LVHW051229080426
835513LV00016B/1493